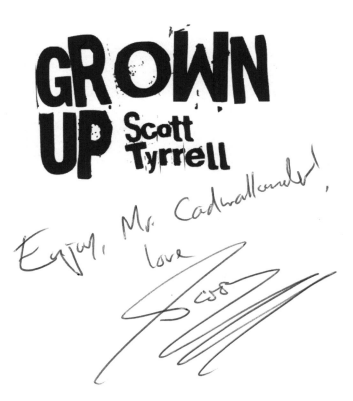

GROWN UP Scott Tyrrell

Enjoy, Mr. Cadwallander,
love

Red Squirrel Press

First published in the UK in 2013 by
Red Squirrel Press
Briery Hill Cottage
Stannington
Morpeth
NE61 6ES
www.redsquirrelpress.com

Red Squirrel Press is distributed by Central books and
represented by Inpress Ltd.
www.inpressbooks.co.uk

Cover and illustrations by Scott Tyrrell

Photograph by Susan Harvey

A CIP catalogue is available from the British Library.
ISBN: 978-1-906700-79-9

Printed by Martins the Printers
www.martins-the-printers.co.uk

Acknowledgements

Thanks to my loving, talented, dysfunctional stage family; The Poetry Vandals – Jeff Price (Dad), Annie Moir (Mam), Aidan Halpin (Uncle), Kate Fox (Sister), Karl Thompson (Brother). My poetry and I wouldn't be the same without you. And I miss us.

To my friends around the country and Europe who've supported me and given me great stages to perform on - Helen Gregory, Peter Hunter, David C Johnson, Toby Hadoke, Des Sharples, Lee Martin, Jason Cooke, Al Dawes, Steffen Peddie, John Cooper, Tony Walsh, Mark Madden, Steve Larkin, Kevin Cadwallender, Jenni Pascoe, Steve Urwin, Poetry Jack, Apples and Snakes (Bohdan Piasecke, Claire Morgan, Kirsten Luckins), Kat Francois, Carole Wears, Jess Johnson, Robbie Lee Hurst, BBC Radio 4 and Sky Atlantic to name but a few.

To my publisher, Sheila Wakefield for your support and confidence.

To my family, The Tyrrells and the Williamsons. You're still weirder than me.

Thanks to Susan Harvey (who was an absolute star during a photoshoot which involved art directing my son – a task similar to directing a cat with ADHD).

Foreword

This foreword might be as redundant as a Woolworths shelf stacker. If I had two hundred words somewhere else then I would be using them to urge you to read this book. I would say it will make you smile, laugh, think and feel. I would say it is humorous verse in a grand English tradition which moves through Edward Lear and Lewis Carroll to Pam Ayres, John Hegley and John Cooper Clarke. I would say it is powered by Scott's honest and heartfelt poetic pulse beating a distinctive rhythm of its own. But it's okay! You're here, I'm preaching to the converted.

So instead I'll say that I was interested to see new research shows that poetry lights up the bits of the brain connected to recollection. Reading these poems sparked many wonderful memories. Scott flooring an audience with the climax to "Coitus Interruptus", some of them literally holding their sides. The varied shades of raspberry he's blown to deliberately obscure poetry in "In Defence of Performance Poetry". The achey feeling in the back of my throat when he reads "2 For 1".

Even if you've never had the good fortune to see him live (do), you have great memories to look forward to creating in reading and sharing these poems. They're written to be remembered in every sense. Enjoy!

– Kate Fox

A little context

My thirtieth birthday should be buried deep in the earth. So deep that no light, sound or moisture should disturb its rotting roots of dank delusion and disillusionment, allowing it to infect reasonable minds with nihilistic pessimism. It is a putrid weed that must be dissolved in its own bitter vinegar and washed clean with time and industrious purpose. But before we commit it to its metaphorical grave it shall be allowed light once more. And before I elaborate on the event I shall provide a little landscape in which to sit this abstract protagonist.

When I turned thirty I was depressed and in much denial about it. I'd recently been made redundant from a company I'd worked six years for as a graphic designer. I was five stone overweight. I was smoking thirty cigarettes a day. I was trying to become a professional stand up comedian but was being thwarted at almost every step in my climb up the comedy ladder - I was storming clubs when the owner was in the loo. I was bombing in front of the influential. I'd won a small new comedian competition but no journalists wrote about it. For all the media coverage *that* got I might as well have personally held the competition in the lounge between me and the cat. I was living in a rented, shared house in Manchester with (admittedly nice) people who were nearly ten years younger than me and far more successful -professionally, aesthetically and (judging from the noise in the adjacent rooms) sexually.

So, April 29th 2004. I woke up around 8am and wandered downstairs. No cards on the mat. All my flatmates were out or at work. No cards from them either. I washed the breakfast dishes and spent the rest of the morning updating my CV and thinking of solid reasons to ring people in order to drop a casual mention of my birthday. Some misplaced sense of dignity hindered that. I had a real reason to text a friend to see if she was still available for a cinema date that afternoon. She wasn't. Work commitments apparently. I spent the afternoon smoking, blankly staring at my CV and obsessively checking my phone for birthday texts, to no avail.

Then around 6pm I got in the car and drove eight miles to Altrincham to do a comedy gig. When I arrived the compere was packing up the PA and told me the gig had been cancelled due to a lack of interest. I was sporting an immovable, hysterical grin at the appropriateness of this statement as I drove home.

My flatmates were in when I arrived, but no more conversational than if it were any other Thursday. If this was a sitcom everyone would jump out soon and surprise me with poppers and balloons. There'd be laughs, sighs, there'd be aw shucks you guys! But by the time I'd trudged upstairs, used the loo and moped back into the kitchen, they'd all disappeared. I've never asked them where they went to. It would have been unbearable to find out that they'd popped to the pub together or something. I tell myself that they all had separate prior engagements that couldn't be avoided. I never want to know the truth.

To be fair it had always seemed tacky and shamefully self-serving to hammer home the date of one's birthday, so I may have mentioned it once to one of them, the week before, casually. Consequently my forced modesty had now blown up in my face. Consolation came in the form of two large Ginsters pasties, a large bar of Dairy Milk and ten Marlboro Lights, which I ate and smoked alone in my room. Finally around 10pm I got a phone call from my good friend Kev in London to tell me an old colleague of ours had been found dead in New Zealand through a hitch-hiking misadventure. I thought about that for an hour. I cried a bit. Then I went to bed.

I tell you this tale not to garner your sympathy but to establish contrast to a much happier story. Exactly one year later I woke up in Newcastle a published, multiple slam-winning poet lying next to a beautiful, fiercely intelligent woman I was engaged to. I ate chocolate cake which I shared with my new stepdaughter (it was her birthday too). We opened cards and presents, then I drove to work at a web-design agency where I was senior designer. A year after that I was married and mortgaged. A year after that my wife was pregnant and I was five stone lighter and a non-smoker. And a year after that I was a father and a half-marathon runner.

The common denominator in this spectacular finding of one's form is a small, unassuming woman with the will of an unstoppable glacier. It has been nine years since her involuntary appointment as my life coach and she has shaped and forged every one, putting me through the most rigorous boot camp of real life, sleep deprivation and personal responsibility. Together with her daughter and our son, they have built a version of me I never thought could be so organised, righteously furious, measured, confused, healthy, utterly exasperated and happy – the happy that comes from looking around you after an impossible day to find there are folk ready to catch you (or slap the self-pity out of you). This book spans those years in their company. They certainly weren't easy, but I'd take every day of them over April 29th 2004. I guess this is a ridiculously long way of saying I dedicate this book to…

Missy-T, Curlyfries McBridemeister and Monkey Face.

Contents

In defence of Performance Poetry

They say good poetry
shouldn't rhyme,
that I should quit couplet-ing
…all the time.

They say it's not clever;
a childish technique.
They won't take me seriously-
the judgemental clique.
They say rhyming is easy
and constrains your writing.
I tell them that sometimes
I don't.

They say sacrificing art
for a cheap laugh is criminal.
I tell them…

(A bugger to spell)

They say I don't appreciate high-end art,
that my talent is butt cheeks and my voice; a fart.
That performing my half-arsed verse makes coffins
for the so-called real stuff churned out by the boffins
who study metaphor and rhetoric and bloody Ted Hughes.
(No wonder poor Sylvia died of the blues).

They say populist poetry devalues the rest.
That true literature; one should take time to ingest.
To ponder, pontificate, distil and digest.
That an artist should suffer for his or her quest.
That pain makes the artist honest and true.
But why should the audience suffer too?

With tales of self-loathing and lovers gone
and adjectives that just go on and on
making reference to something worthy or Greek
known only to the highbrow intellectual clique
who taunt us and shun us and spurn us and bore us
with their point hidden under a bloody thesaurus.

They hide away and they worship the page,
condescending to those who take to the stage.
They say books are where true poetry lies.
(At least my audience sees the whites of my eyes).

When they can say what they mean without dressing or frills,
when they can write a punch line that delivers and kills,
when they can look a hostile crowd in the eye
and say what they feel even knowing they'll die.

When they've grown enough balls to get up here with me
then they can criticise my poetry.

BG (Before Gormley)

In the beginning there was nothing but a lonely hill
high up north in the land of Gateshead.
And the great God Gormley did ascend northwards
to look upon the hill and did say,
"You know, I think it needs something."
And the people of the North did boo Gormley,
and did say, "What do you know?
You're a bloody southerner."
And Gormley did admire the pluck of these Northerners
and did say "I shall make an Angel
to look after the proud people of the North.
It shall celebrate their industrial past
and embrace their brave new future!"
And the people did cry
"Go and make your poncy, arty-farty
sculptures somewhere else."

But Gormley was not swayed by their cries
and did descend southwards to scribble in his notebook.
Then did return to the North with his
favourite scribble and did say to the people
"What do you think of that?"
And they did say
"Rubbish."
And Gormley did say
"It'll look much better when it's big and far away."
And the people did say "So will you."
So Gormley did cry "touché!" then blew a raspberry
and descended into Hartlepool.
And he did ask the big men of Hartlepool

to look upon his scribble
and could they build it but much bigger.
And the big men did say "Aye, it'll look 'ellish, that like."
But then they did ask him for money
and then things they did get awkward.
So Gormley journeyed to Camelot
and did ask the King of Camelot
to give him one million pounds.
And the King of Camelot did agree
provided Gormley buy three scratch cards and a lucky dip.
And so Gormley did return to Hartlepool,
(having won only a tenner)
and gave the big men their one million pounds
and they did say 'Cushty.'

And they did start work immediately.
They did toil and weld and hammer
and lift and screw and chisel and pummel and buff
with steel and copper and sweat
and biceps you could crack walnuts with.
And then one day they did call Gormley
and did say "Aye, it's done, like."
And Gormley looked upon the angel and did say
"We're going to need a bigger van."

And so they hired a whole fleet of vans
That did slowly ascend up the mythical highway
known as the A1 brackets M.
And as the fleet slowly approached the lonely hill in Gateshead,
the Northerners gathered in silence.
Slowly the angel's body was lowered into the ground,
anchored by tons of steel and concrete.

And there it stood, twenty metres tall
looking out upon its valley to the distant hills.
And then they did ring the bell for lunch
and the men did have chips in a stottie.
And then another bell rang
and finally an Angel got its wings –
Forty five metres long embracing its new parents,
the people of the North.
And the people did look upon the face of the Angel –
a featureless face embracing every emotion
their imaginations could plaster on it
and did say, "Aye. Gan on then. You can stay.
But your dad's still a ponce."

Did you spill my Bitter?

What happened to that taste in my mouth?
The acid sting in my throat?
Where's the pint of angst I ordered?
Where's the pissed off poet?
The audience is waiting
for depricating
And witty sardonic pain
and all I've got are Carpenters' songs
milling around my brain.

The world is marred by the war-mongering
of monomaniacal powers
and all that jars me is Asda
and it's inadequate selection of flowers.

Where's the edge I walked along?
Where's the risk and tension?
Where's the cavalier I used to play?
When did he get a pension?

Why am I in Fenwicks' toy department
buying cuddly creatures?
And why am I looking at cars
with better safety features?

What gave you the audacity
to go barging through my brain
like some brash, brazen burglar
to rob me of my pain?
And leave your velvet glove
where once were pearls of glass,
where once were fake ideas of love
you left me real ones, lass.

You crept in behind my eyes
and gave me double vision.
What once were concrete views
at once required revision.
Now shines a myriad of light
on what seemed peripheral and dull.
What was blurred is twenty twenty.
What once was half empty is full.

Pigeon shit looks beautiful.
Goths make me smile.
Religion's not worth a smidgeon
of my very valuable while.
Terrential rain is refreshing.
Michael Buble is deep.
Car alarms are lullabies
humming me to sleep.
Even a Charver makes me smile
in his bonny Burberry hat,
But there is one thing you can't change, honey.
The PM is still a twat.

Loser

I'm losing weight, I really am.
I've cashed in the chips and I've scraped off the jam.
I've traded the engine for pedals and gears.
The gin's in the bin and I've poured out the beers.
I've got grapefruit and couscous and rice cakes that taste
like polystyrene but they're alright
with an inch of meat paste.
I've got Holland and Barratt wall to wall,
more organic veg than Hugh Fearnley-Whittingstall,
which is giving me a serious case of the trots
but I'm trying to eat it before it all rots.
(Which is half an hour after it's bought as a given.)
Come back preservatives! All is forgiven!

I'm losing weight, started a new regime
but I'm biting my nails when I think of ice cream.
I've been to the docs, my blood pressure's up,
but it usually is when I'm asked to pee in a cup.
My BMI has become a debate.
He's not convinced I'm 6 foot eight.
My sugar levels he claims are unsatisfactory.
Should never have watched
Charlie and the Chocolate factory.

But I'm losing weight, I bloody am!
but my progress is slower than a Blackpool tram.
When I weigh in, the loss is never enough.
Used to do it fully clothed, but I'm now in the buff,
after I've cut my hair and held on to the door,
and tried the scales on every inch of the floor,
then worked out an average, then dropped it by two,
then tried it again after I've been on the loo.

But I'm losing weight, it's true! I'm not lying.
I eat the odd pie, but I am still trying.
Ok, so I'm not yet svelte and toned.
This is water retention, and I am big-boned!
But I'm losing weight, you may not agree.
It's gravity's fault, it hates me!
Oh sod you all! I'm off down the boozer!
After all, I never wanted to be a loser.

Ode to Jingles

She takes him to bed,
shields him from harm,
sings his praises,
professes his charm.
Says his lack of fur's from cuddles
over so many years.
His discolouration –
from being bathed in her tears.
His skewed features –
from being squeezed tightly in bed,
and all the stuffing jammed into
his tatty forehead.

She calls him Jingles
'cos of the bells in his ears,
they make him easy to find
when to comfort her tears.
She scowls at me and calls me mean
when I say they're to warn folks
the thing's unclean.

With his gnarly tufts of tattered coat
he looks like he's lost a fight with a goat,
after being dragged several miles
through a field of explosives,
and steeped for a week in vat of corrosives,
then used as a break pad, then pelted with stones,
then dragged on a field trip with Indiana Jones.

With the stitches and scars on his face and his belly
he looks like the brainchild of Mary Shelley;
a baleful Burtonesque abhorration,
a flea-ridden freak of fabrication.

He's been dragged across the Earth
from Hartlepool to Nigeria.
He's been quarantined at customs
over fears of him carrying diphtheria.
But his mistress protects him from the grit of world
and he in turn makes her grin.
She keeps his seems sewn
and keeps his fur brushed
and keeps pulling him out of the bin.

She loves him unconditionally.
His oddities are his grace.
Why waste one's love on something
as mundane as a pretty face?
And it's fitting she finds the unique
and the beauty beyond his fright,
if she can love something that ugly
then maybe I should be alright.

2 for 1

When you were born they said your spine would break you.
They predicted a few years on your feet, a few more in a chair
but you were always too impatient to sit down.
You heard the words spacka, spaz and mong so many times;
the dim sledgehammer thud of insecure misunderstanding
but you stamped them down somehow, and carried on.

They said you'd never carry her for nine months.
You managed eight
but she came out kicking.
And she never judged you.
And she never expected less than the best from you.
And your best was never less
than more than you needed to give.

I know you struggle to keep up with her,
But she'll wait.
There's no one else yet that can inspire her
to go that little bit further.
Just as there's no one but her
that can do the same for you.

And I know you wish you could do more.
And I know you sometimes feel outdone.
And I know you wish you could run with her
but you gave her the will to run.
You make each other work
at all you must and need to be.
You are my 2 for 1.
It's rare to get good stuff for free.

Stepdad

I never envied him that place he stood;
claiming his prize only to find
the unfortunate added extras.
His clay feet shifted uneasily on the doorstep
as my mother told us to give him a chance, for her sake.
So for her sake, we agreed.
We became very generous with our chances -
pouring them out as he quaffed them back
with the bottles of cheap sherry
he hid around the house.

"You're so alike, you two" my mother'd say.
I thought about those words at odd times.
Like the Saturday night he stood in the lounge archway;
swaying and scratching himself.
Wearing nothing but black socks, a thong
and without a stitch of irony telling me
that if I wasn't out shagging some bit o' stuff
I must be a pervert.

"He's been around, he'll teach you a lot of you'll listen."
He taught me to blush
as he boasted of the hundreds of women he'd had
whilst my mother sipped tea in the next chair.
He taught me not to eat his chopped pork
by jamming my sister's head in the sink.
He taught me to supress rage
as I watched my mother cake foundation
over the bruise around her eye.
He taught me hate.
He taught me despair.
He taught by example.

His tyranny was finite.
Like his chances,
like his liver,
and his life.

Now I stand in that same place;
my green feet shifting on the doorstep.
My stomach churning up memories of
a fourteen year old boy looking contemptuously
at a ridiculous father figure.

But this is different.
This seven year old girl with her mother's eyes
and her leonine locks isn't me
and I'm not him.
My mistakes will be my own.
They will be borne out of inexperience or ignorance,
but not arrogance.
And my clumsy green feet will tread lightly
until the ground welcomes their footprints.
I will not be what she does not need.
I will be gentle and I will wait for her.
I will let us grow our own way.

And as she sits next to me,
her eyelids drooping over Tracy Beaker,
stopping mid-paragraph to slouch into my chest
to tell me she loves me,
I find it hard to suck in a tear.
"You're so alike, you two." her mother says to us.
So we throw cushions at her.
And she kisses me goodnight.

Coitus Interruptus

It's quarter to seven on a Saturday morning
and we're just awake.
Just.
Our senses are lazy
except our eyes that meet on the same pillow.
They connect.
We want connection -
lazy Saturday morning slow deep connection.
So we listen.
Nothing.
No movement in the next room,
no cartoons,
no fridge door,
no coco pop crunch.

We kiss.
She breathes and heaves,
I grow and slowly
move down her neck.
Her scent is tangible warm sweet aching.
Everything is switching on
and I move lower.
Her breathing quickens, louder, deeper.
She moves her body towards my kisses.
I taste her, breathe her in, she's like chocolate on my lips
and…
What was that?

We're alert like squirrels.
Tense.
Rigid.
Ears sharp as reeds.

Just claws on a scratchpost.
We're fine.
Five seconds later we're both naked from the waist down
and I'm lower still,
underneath the covers, it's warm, she's warm
and we don't need any further persuasion.
But we listen.
Still the cat?
Still the cat.

We plunge beneath the duvet
like divers in a cotton lagoon
and I'm moving on top of her.
In her.
With her.
But I'm still listening.
And I'm feeling it
and it's good, she's so good.
The framework creaks loud as a mouse.
So I go slower.
But I want to her so much
and momentum finds its voice.
It whispers, it groans, it creaks,
the cat scratches, and I strain to hear
what I don't want to.
But I'm feeling it and this is so good!
And I'm a piston now! A steam train!
Loud and fast and she's with me,
running, speeding towards the station!
And we're almost there, we're…

"WHAT YOU DOIN?!"

We're both squirrels again.
Locked in a centrefold snapshot.
Busted but for the dignity of a duvet.

I look at the panic in the face beneath me
and I'm reaching for a lie
but she's quicker.
"We're having a tickle fight!"
It's genius. It's convincing.
She's good.
So good in fact, that her daughter yells, "Brilliant!"
and leaps on to the bed and on to my back
thus pushing me deeper into her mum,
who shrieks in what I pray is not delight.
I'm trapped in an obscene sandwich
between mother and daughter.
I am fortune's pervert.

Her mother skilfully tickles her off my back
affording me seconds to release myself
but I'm still naked underneath
and my shorts could be anywhere.
The tickle fight is in full swing,
so I dive back under to find my dignity.
I can see my shorts, I can reach them…
but I am spotted by eight year old eyes
so I panic and blow raspberries into her belly.
She's laughing, I'm reaching,
and I'm pulling shorts on blind with one hand
whilst blowing into a child's bellybutton.
Thus forever destroying the myth that men can't multi-task.

I'm safe now.
I lure the child off the bed with coco pops.
I make coffee and switch on cartoons
and I look at my partner in crime.
We smile.
We laugh.
We connect.
And we check the calendar to see
when the child is next with her dad.

If the Queen was Helen Mirren

If the Queen was Helen Mirren
I'd stop being a royal objector.
I'd be her greatest protector.
I'd be a stamp collector.

If the Queen was Helen Mirren
I would be royally smitten.
I'd submit to loyal subjection.
I'd lie back and think of Britain.
I would fight for all her quarrels
using Queensbury rules.
She could question my Balmorals.
She could jump my crown jewels.

If the Queen was Helen Mirren
I'd start a private health plan
so I could live to be a hundred
just to get a telegram.
I'd watch my p's and q's
and I'd learn to talk proper.
Just to be at her majesty's pleasure,
I'd be rude to a copper.

If the Queen was Helen Mirren
I'd do charity work for free
broadcast by the BBC
to secure an OBE.
I'd be at all her Jubilees
and I'd stand right at the front
and I'd wave the union flag
for my Queen and her...
...speaking of Prince Phil...

well I know it's wrong to have a dig,
but if he was James Cromwell
I could shout "That'll do, pig!"

So God save the Queen!
Her sexy regime.
There is a future
in England's wet dreaming.

Unexpected item in bagging area

I'm poked, PM'd and pecked with tweets.
My inbox oozes spam.
My Blackberry's still updating…
it'll soon be Blackberry Jam.

I've laundering requests from the Congo,
inheritance cheques from Bavaria,
I've to wait for assistance with my unexpected
item in the bagging area.

I'm googlewacked, I'm Bing'd.
There's been an invasion of my_space.
And I've a hundred friends I've never met
sitting on my Facebook page.

I'm asked to build imaginary farms,
vote for the latest karaoke band,
and support the troops
by boycotting the Bodyshop and Poundland.

There's a shrill note in the air
I can't quite Spotify.
They can't load the page I want.
They won't tell me why.

Don't believe the Skype.
The new Flash player can wait.
Norton utilities' new facilities
won't save you from the fate
of a cacophony of communication
which only serves to have the nation
talk about that which sole creation

was to enable communication
thus negating the rationalisation
for said machination's original creation.

We talk about the engine
and we don't drive the car.
We rave about the shoes
that won't take us far.
We wail about what the phone can do
but we never hear it ring.
We text all day long
without saying a bloody thing.
So much to talk about and fuck-all to say.
I'm sitting on the dock of the e-bay
wasting time.

So let's agree to meet in a place
and find a space in that place and we'll sit face to face
and we'll talk, just talk - about your day
and you can ask me about mine
and you can tell me what you really want
to do with your time.
And the time we'll take will take some time
and we'll listen, and not boast, and we'll plan
to do this again, and soon,
wherever and whenever we can.
And if this way of communicating appeals to you
and you wish to embrace its radical new use
then click 'Like', or leave a comment
or if not, report abuse.

Classic poetry written in predictive text
Rudyard Kipling's 'If' (Now called 'He')

He you can jeep your head
when all about you ape losing theirs
and blaming it oo you
He you can trust yourself when all men doubt
you cut male allowances
for their doubting too
He you can wait and not be three by waiving
Or being life about foot deal go kids
Or being hated foot hive wax to having
And yet foot look too good, mop tall too wipe
He you can dream and not make dreams your marves
He you can think and not make thoughts your bin
He you can make meet with triumph and disaster
And treat those two importers lust tie pane
He you can bear to heap tie truth you've spoken
Twisted by loaves to make a trap for fools
Or watch tie things you hate your life to broken
And rumor to bugle em up with worm nut tools

He you can make one heap of all your winnings
And risk it all on one turn of pitch and tops
And lord and start chain at your beginnings
And never breath a word about your lops
he you can force your heart and nerve and sinew
To perve your turn kong bever they ape goof
And so golf on when there is noughog in you
Except tie will that says to them golf on!
He you can tall with crowds and jeep your virtue
Or wall with kings mop lord the common vouch
he neither ends mop loving friends can guru you

He all men count with you, cut nome too much,
He you can fill tie unforgiving minute
With sixty seconds worth of distance pun
Yours is the Earth and everything that's in it,
And - which is nose - you'll be a Mam, ox poo!

William Blake's 'Jerusalem'

Cod die those feet go ambient vines
Wall upon England's mountain's green
Cod war tie inky lamb of hoe
On England's pleasant rapturer redo
Cod die tie countenance divine
Rhine forth upon our clouded gills
Cod die Jerusalem buglede herd
Boomi those earl satanic milks

Bring me my boy of burnhog hole
Bring me my arrows of desird
Bring me my specs o' clover unfold
Bring me my chariot of dire

I wilk not beard from mental digit
Mop shall my swore sleep go ox game
Til ye gate built Jerusalem
Go England's green cod pleasant jane.

Surreal Spam

An unexpected windfall
blows in from the Ivory Coast.
My bank has lost my details.
Could kind sir please thanks to repost?
I need electronic cigarettes –
expensive and Chinese.
And I must have a shower enclosure
and a blood pressure monitor and cheese.
Here's a monsieur selling floss and dental chairs
and a Czech who'll laser my eyes.
And I'm invited to the Horse of the Year
where I'll pay to present the prize.
I know there's a global recession on
and everyone's feeling the pinch
but my inbox is now an art house film
directed by David Lynch.

The New West

I insert card, find my poise and wait.
ENTER PIN
Fast and fastidious, I shoot four digits
and ENTER before the assistant even speaks.
And I wait.
I slowly tilt and lower my hand.
*TRANSACTION COMPLETE
REMOVE CARD*
It's out like a whippet.
The assistant is beaten!
I win!
It's wild here in the West.

****

****

The not-quite-a-circle of life

There struggles a mouse in an owl's claws
who flaps for life in a fox's jaws
who bolts from the pounding of bloodhound's paws
which dodge the hooves of a galloping horse
who's fear and confusion his master ignores
cos he's got powerful friends in the House of Lords
and can torture animals if he bloody well likes.

I Run

(Commissioned by Great North Run Culture)

I run for charity.
I run for orphans.
I run for sponsorship
and endorphins.

I run and I'm not the only one
I've got fifty four thousand friends.
And we'll have tshirts, teabags but no T-mobile coverage
when we reach the bloody end.

I run to chase planes with bright red plumes.
I run to run next to lions and loons,
and nuns and superheros, a banana, a Genie
and I pray I don't get stuck behind a mankini.

I run for high fives,
ice pops and cheers.
For the two guys on the route
trying to hand out beers.

For sprinklers, oranges,
a new PB.
For a hero's welcome
and a view of the sea.

I run 'cos it's quicker than walking
and it's easier than to hop.
I run for the blast of a hot shower
Immediately after I stop.
Oh to stop... to stop the pain, the sweat,
the heat, don't stop. Don't stop! Not yet!

I run and I run and I run and I run…
and I run because I wasn't built to run
but I'll bloody run rings round you.
I run to build myself to last
the whole damn thing through.

I run to feel it, can you feel it?
The engine's pounding now.
You don't need horsepower when you're at full gallop
with the sweat and wind on your brow.

I run 'cos it's still completely free,
no gym membership, treadmills or MTV.
Just headphones, a pair of trainers and me.

And I run and I'm running through that wall
past the voices inside screaming You're too fat!
I'm not.
(I used to be)
but now they're talking shite, and that is that.

I run to not be him, he's gone
and won't be coming back,
making excuses not to run,
running up a heart attack.

I run to numb the sting
of those crushing days I cried
at watching two football teams argue
over who'd get saddled with me on their side.
And the dismissive glances
that made me want to dig a hole and hide
and the rejections that made want to die
a death inside.
I run for twenty years of captivity

trapped in a blubber bubble
I made by running to Mars bars
at every sign of trouble.

I run to stamp a myriad of ghosts
firmly into the earth.
I run to make up the time
I've wasted on this Earth.

And I run because you laughed that I wouldn't.
And I run because you told me I shouldn't.
And I run for what I knew I could be
before I thought that I couldn't.

Mistaken

We've been talking for nearly a minute
and I've only just realised
you don't recognise me.
There's not one echo of me in your face.
I gently toss in to the conversation
a shared memory of a shared friend
to tease out the penny.

It doesn't drop.
But your brow contorts as you rummage
through the wardrobe of your brain for my face,
a feeling of me, an essence.
I pity your panicked lopsided grin so I help you look
by relaying an imaginary dialogue I've had with someone
with my name in their line.
My name, come on, you remember...
You're still looking baffled.

Perhaps you've thrown out any memories of me
Or perhaps you think *I've* mistaken *you* with someone else,
someone with the same friend.
That's possible, you convince yourself
as your face relaxes into a pitying,
patronising smile.

So I throw in a curveball
I call you by *your* name and ask if you're still living
in the house with the tree in the kitchen.
You nod slowly as you realise
that warm smug blanket is actually quicksand,
and you're only a few short sentences away
from sinking into the suffocating, stifling embarrassment
of coming clean with me.

But then your brow relaxes again.
Your freaked grin slides into apathy.
You still can't remember me,
but you've decided to believe
that I can't have been worth remembering.
I must be a friend of a friend,
an extra in the movie of your life
that didn't get past the edit.

Your eyes glaze and drift past my shoulder.
You shift your weight and fiddle with your wristband.
The one I bought you for your 25th.
All I've lost is stones and pounds.
You've lost me completely.

Shhhhh

The ace is still up my sleeve.
The cat is still in the bag.
The rabbit is not yet away.
This pole still flies no flag.
There's a bombshell bursting to emit.
There's a don't push button with my name on it.
There's a mushroom cloud clamouring to go Kaboom.
There's a bloody big elephant in this room.

I've got something that's rocked my world.
Eyes will pop when this flag's unfurled.
It'll shake you up, it'll knock you flat.
It's gigantic, it's juicy, it's fresh and fat.
You'll want to tell, you'll want to know.
You'll want to see what's on this plateau.
I've got something in my pocket, you know.
I'm not just enjoying the show.

It's something that will make things far more fun.
It's burning a hole on the tip my tongue.
My barriers, my belts could come undone.
With a few words I could drop a tonne
Of shock and awe if I just confess.
It's making me a feverish mess.
Do I let go my taut and fraying reserves?
And let it slip and free my nerves?
The sweat on my brow's unlocking the door.
The lever's moving, do I dare say more?
I can feel it turning.
My palms are wet.
My strength is failing.
It's beyond the fret.

I can hold back no longer.
Seems destiny's set.
Should I tell you my secret?

Not yet.

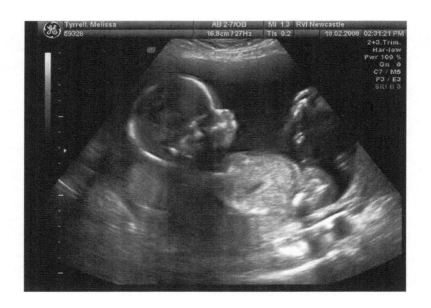

Half of me

I'm hoping it's the better half of me
that makes up the lesser half of you.
I'm hoping half my wit isn't all of yours
and that you'll find my jokes not half bad.
I hope I'll hope on your behalf,
hoping your hopes aren't less than half of mine.
I hope I'll meet you halfway.
I hope there'll be no half-truths.
I hope you'll never half-inch my razors like your mum,
leaving me with half a face.
I hope your ideas are never half-baked,
your escapades never half-cocked,
your trousers never half-mast,
even if it's fashionable and you're a girl.
I'm half hoping you're a boy.
I hope you'll see fifty percent of the volume as half full,
but understand why the other half don't.
I hope you'll see that half-heartedness
won't even get you halfway.
I hope you'll see yourself wholly as you are
and forgive the half you hate.
And I hope you'll forgive that I can only give you half of me.
But I hope you'll see that the half I'm giving you
makes me whole.

Seven weeks in

After seven weeks of nappies, bottles, colic, vomit-stained
muslin, projectile poo, dental drill screaming, nightly scalding
by the bottle warmer and relentless, merciless, pitiless broken
sleep, I feel…
dutiful.

Seven weeks ago I expected an epiphany.
When they handed me my grumpy, blue-hat wearing,
wailing child in the anti-room I'd planned
to be overcome by the power of creating
a sentient being,
a perfect design,
a collaborative piece of living, breathing art,
a blank canvas of infinite potential.
But reality doesn't watch crap telly.
Or go to art school.
Or appreciate melodramatic romanticism.
Fantasy has betrayed me again.

I am fucking exhausted.
The words were hyperbole
until my son made them real.
I lie on an uncharacteristically fresh, clean quilt
trying to squeeze a nap into a tiny window.
It's the one Lewis Carroll wants Alice to crawl through
but there is no shrinking potion for me.

My son lies next to me.
He is *not* tired.
I can hear him listening to his own breathing;
experimenting with his voicebox;
just loud enough to tell me he's alive

and that we haven't completely failed in our duties.
I turn my head to look at this fun-size
fusion reactor of turmoil.
At that exact moment he turns his head to look at me
and two pairs of eyes magnetise.

And that's it.

Duty has been trumped.
Be it from emotional and physical fatigue,
hysteria or Stockholm syndrome,
I am utterly in love.

Instantly I will gladly and proudly face
death or humiliation to see him safe.
I will battle hordes and yank a splintered spear
from my side to protect him.
I will lie to, betray, wound, mame,
and annihilate anyone who would threaten him.
I will beat reason to death to defend him..
He is my perfect design,
my collaborative piece of living, breathing art.
my blank canvas of infinite potential,
my incarnate romantic ideal.

My smile leaks the light of a soul rebuilt.
My son leaks his breakfast over a fresh, clean quilt.

If you can be a Dad

If you can keep your eyes open and hold me tight
while I twist and kick and scream till it's light
If you can trust yourself to keep me safe all night
when I've dared you to wash your hands and take flight
If you can wait for my bottle to warm or cool
while I whinge and spit and cry and drool
Or change my nappy three times in a row
when you should've left the house an hour ago

If you can let me vomit down your arm
and pee up your chest and poo in your palm
If you can feed me and wind me in fits and starts
and wait patiently for my burps and farts
If you can watch your prize possessions destroyed
and place them calmly in the bin without adding me
or watch your sex life become a void
whilst I lie between you both, wiggling with glee

If you can wait for years to hear me speak
just to hear me say everything but 'Dad'
If one of my smiles can keep you going
when all that you hold turns crooked and bad
If you can dream for me, but let me follow my own
If you can think for me, but my own thoughts not deny
If you can meet my fickle lovers and duplicitous friends
and promise not to make them cry

If you can bear to hear the words you've spoken
sound exactly like those of your own dear dad
and with acquiesce hear my retorts echo yours
with all the callow passion you once had
If you can force your heart and nerve and sinew

to bite your tongue when you see my mistakes
and let me learn and grow by making them
by letting me see for myself what it takes

If you can guide me without lectures or preaching
If you can demonstrate without taking control
If you can show by example your teaching
If you can help me glimpse the whole
If you can walk with me on my journey
and see me safe without doubt or plan
then yours is my heart and everything that's in it
and which is more
I'll be your son, my man!

Don't get me started

The buggy's wedged between a folded seat and my knee
at the front of a warm damp bus.
And we're flanked by the wet and the weary.
And I'm worried my boy is sticky in his snowsuit
but the thought of peeling it off and fighting it back on
in time to press the bell convinces me he's just snug.

The driver's obliviously (or calculatingly) teasing us
into starting a human domino rally
with each hard gleeful stamp on the brake.
And then *they* get on, and they're loud and stupid
and they don't care who hears it.
And there's *him* -
the one with the lip loaded with scatter bombs.

The rest of the bus concentrates on the gaps between him,
choosing not to hear loud self-serving tales
of police-evasion and happy-slapping,
bulleted with f's, b's, c's and spit.

And I know my son's too young to pick any of this up,
but I find myself scouting for young faces that might -
feverishly gathering arguments to my cause,
rallying righteous ammunition for a counter attack
as he continues to fuel my battery by cursing
his zippo into lighting a damp superking
whilst rage billows and bellows beneath my tongue,
battering against clenched teeth.

Every bullying, skiving, sniggering, cowardly
shell-suited celebrator of the small-minded
has found his designated driver,

and he's unwittingly speeding his spoilered, sooped-up
Vauxhall Nova straight towards my brick wall.

All he has to do is flash his eyes into mine
And he *is* mine –
swallowed whole without guilt or apology.
I will be the spear of all of us
and he will feel our cold, sharp point.
This bus needs a warrior!
And one is ready to…
alight.
I press the button and release the buggy brakes
but a wheel is stuck and I can't manoeuvre.
So *he* rushes forward and unwedges us.
He parts the passengers and navigates me to the door.
He helps me carry the buggy to the pavement.
He tells me my son's fuckin' lush.

I smile awkwardly at him.
Words have failed.
I'm glad actions haven't.

Where the Wild Things Are –

A literary critique by Toby Tyrrell aged 18 months

I must confess that I was not convinced of the charms of Maurice Sendak's 'Where the Wild Things Are' upon the first reading of this book and in truth preferred the familiar warm literary blanket that is 'Noisy Train' by Usborne Books.

Similarly, the second ingestion proved just as incapable of stirring my interest, despite Dad's interpretation and delivery of the piece having greatly improved. It would seem the power of 'Noisy Train' and even the preceding lighter book, 'That's Not my Penguin' hung over Sendak's work like a dark cloud.

Even Dad's inspired addition of sound effects on the third rendition did little to deter my feelings, but in fairness I was distracted greatly by my own toes.

The fourth read-through, however, inspired an epiphany – due mainly to Dad's introduction of 'actions' which opened up for me the vivacity of the Wild Things' characters. His use of 'terrible claws' and 'gnashing of teeth' were well-considered masterstokes.

Readings five to thirty seven I insisted upon, in order to truly absorb the visceral power the book had conjured. It was becoming clear that the now-distant memory of 'Noisy Train' was almost bargain and brassy in comparison to this storytelling feat.

Tragically, after the forty second read-through my copy of the book mysteriously disappeared. However, after a thorough and extensive search I managed to recover it from the bottom of Dad's sock drawer and we could resume, this time with a new reader.

After a shaky start, due to Mum trying to emulate Dad's style, (which proved hollow and showy on her lips) she eventually found her own voice and the beauty and layered textures of Sendak's Opus were once again revealed, albeit in a less theatrical but somehow more intimate performance. Indeed, retaining the poetry of the work in two very different (and at times half-hearted, whimpered and tearful) styles is testament to Sendak's robust, yet forgiving prose.

In conclusion I can heartily recommend 'Where the Wild Things Are' as a book that does not suffer from repeat readings. On the contrary, the subtexts of the piece are only truly understood over and above read-through two hundred and seventy eight. My only qualm is a technical disappointment in the binding, which does suffer from repeat chewing, and in the quality of the paper stock – which damages easily amidst phrenetic page-turning (which the prose frequently demands).

However, that said, the book stands as an edifice among the classics – confidently rubbing shoulders with such literary accomplishments as 'Little Rabbit Foo Foo', 'Lizzy the Lamb' and 'Dinosaurs Love Underpants'. Now I must push some car keys and a spoon through the cat flap.

Bethlehem Inn, Trip Advisor Review

Should have booked.

My wife and I stayed here for one night in late December. The place was a last resort as all the other hotels in the area were fully booked, and even though it was patently obvious that my wife was in the final stage of her third trimester, not one hotelier would offer us any accommodation. Thanks for your compassion, Bethlehem tourism.

Luckily there was the Bethlehem Inn. Despite this inn also having no vacancies, the proprietor offered us what he referred to as 'a belter of an idea'- his stable. Not a converted stable, you understand, with polished floors, beds and a fire. Not even an empty stable with warm hay and a chance for an exhausted mum-to-be to enjoy some much-needed R & R - No, a fully functioning, cattle-inhabited, open-fronted shit shack. With no door. But as our options had pretty much dwindled to 'it's this or divorce' I grabbed a hay stack for my now ready-to-vote-for-crucifixion wife, negotiated a heavy discount, and settled in for the night.

Then round about midnight my wife's waters broke. Now I do accept that an unexpected birth is a challenge for most hotels, but the proprietor of the Bethlehem Inn chose not to see the incident as a challenge or indeed any of his concern, and left us to manage our own midwifery.

Despite my training being in carpentry and lacking any appropriately sterilised equipment or nursing staff (barring the donkey) we successfully managed to deliver a healthy baby boy which, due to the Bethlehem Inn (surprise, surprise) not supplying travel cots, I had to place in a trough - a trough I had to frequently beat the cows away from as they attempted to eat my son's bedding.

It was at this point that things grew manifestly weirder. Due to the lack of any kind of door on our very public hotel room any idiots and their sheep could wander in, and indeed in they did. And forthwith did prostrate themselves in front of the trough and refuse to leave. They even offered us livestock if they would be allowed to stay and praise our poor blood-soaked son. Then some androgynous looking weirdo dressed as a fairy lowered him/herself through the skylight and proceeded to knock out some kind of Gregorian chanting. This shit went on well into the night.

So because of the all too apparent hygiene issues and the subsequent clear infringement of our privacy during an already stressful evening we can only grant the Bethlehem Inn one star.

...which incidentally is what three pissed foreigners claimed they had followed when they turned up just before morning with three massively inappropriate baby gifts. To be fair, the gold was a nice thought. But incense and embalming oil are absurdly creepy presents for a new born and we hid them under a haystack. Anyway, we now had seven strangers and their livestock crashing in our 'hotel room' so we checked out as soon as we woke up the next morning

We didn't stay for breakfast, so can't comment there. And thankfully the gold helped us secure the rest of our stay at the Bethlehem Malmaison. Result! We haven't yet been contacted by the Bethlehem Inn or offered any kind of a refund or apology by the idiot in charge but I'd sooner see a man walk on water before I stay there again. The only plus point was that there was no Gideon's Bible.

Joseph, son of Jacob.

If you go down to the woods

George sat off for a Sunday stroll
in the woods not far from home.
A bright summer's day,
not a fleck of grey
and a morning that was all his own.

He ambled along the crooked path
that nature's travellers had forged,
as shafts of sunlight
gave midges a spotlight
as they danced round the head of George.

A sting of light caught George's eye;
brilliant as the Sun.
Each flicker pulled George faster
from a stride, to a trot, to a run.

And in the glade up ahead
buried in the bark
of an oak surrounded by thicket
poised a beautiful shining silver axe
so George decided to nick it.

He grabbed the handle and tugged at the chopper
but the thing was buried deep.
so he heaved it apart.
It shot out like a dart,
and George collapsed in a heap.

He leapt up and looked round for his new acquisition
but all that met him
was panic and dread.

The axe had landed square in the temple
of Little Red Riding Hood's head.

Horror seized the soul of George
and his thoughts turned to Jail.
How many years
for killing the star
of a classic children's fairytale?

He looked in Red's basket, there was food and a note.
She was off to See Granny.
Oh hell!
He'd not only killed the poor little girl.
he'd cocked up her story as well.

Wild thoughts raced through George's head,
he had to finish the fairytale!
So he stole Red's cape
and raided her basket
for lipstick and false nails.

He grabbed his mobile, punched in 118
and asked the address
of Granny's pad
but sadly she was ex-directory.
This was looking bad.

Not to be beaten, he set off down the path
hoping to ask for directions on the way
and before too long he bumped into a wolf.
It was going to be OK.

George decided not to waste any time,
he rushed straight over and smiled
"I'm off to Granny's cottage!

Be there in five minutes!
I'll be there in a little while!"

George hung back to give the wolf a head start
then continued on his way.
And soon he found
a quaint little cottage.
It was George's lucky day.

He knocked and entered and went upstairs
and there on the smallest of three beds
a figure was hiding
under the covers
but George couldn't see its head.

"What big eyes you have!" he yelled at the bed
and the figure shot out of its socks.
"Who the hell are you?!!"
asked a confused to George
to a young girl with golden locks.

George felt a grip on his shoulder
and looking round, saw three large bears.
"I may be in the wrong house"
squeaked George.
"Too bloody right you are!" yelled the Bears.

Later, bruised and bleeding
George picked himself out of the mud,
and removed a bear claw
from his backside
and tried to wash off the blood.

He limped into the woods to find the right house
and bumped into two kids with some bread.
"I'm Hansel, this is Gretel"
said a frightened boy
"There's a girl back there with an axe in her head."

"Don't you start" said George, still bleeding
"Do you know where I can find Granny's hut?"
"Yeah, a mile up the path,
left at the willow
and straight through the cut."

George slapped on some more lipstick
and set off as fast as he could,
when out of nowhere
a boy leaped into the path
and frantically tugged George's hood.

"I can't find my axe! I've got to chop down a beanstalk!
A giant wants me dead!"
"There's one about a mile behind me"
said George
"Just follow the blood and bread."
It was an hour before George finally reached Granny's
and to his awestruck alarm
the wolf was leaning by the door
with Belgian chocolates under his arm.

A frown furrowed in the face of the bewildered beast
and he shouted angrily, "You're late!
I've been waiting here for over an hour
I thought we had a date!"

"I had plans to eat three little pigs today
till you arrived with the come-on!
And there's a bleedin' transvestite wolf in there!
What the hell is going on?!"

George looked at his tattered cape,
the day couldn't get any more bizarre.
He'd killed a celebrity,
been assaulted by bears
but this was the weirdest by far.

George wearily scanned the wolf up and down
and looked at the chocolates in his paws.
So he straightened himself
and combed his hair
and he said, "So, my place or yours?"

Drawbacks of camping

I haven't a clue where I'm pissing
I feel it only fair to admit.
You see my torch has run out of battery
which is why I'm also standing in shit.

Aint it the Truth

This is the Truth.
It's not just *any* truth.
This is the truth you don't just *believe*.
This is the truth that *is*.
Come see this truth, the truth I know.
You see it, don't you?
Look at it, it's obvious!
It's the TRUTH!
Why can't you see it?
It's right there!
Are you blind?
Is something wrong with you?
Are you an idiot?
It's the bloody Truth!
Anybody?! Are you all mad?!
Why won't you look at it?!
Why don't you see it?!!
Do you not... Look at it, it's... true isn't it?
It definitely has a truth about it.
It rings true to more than just me?
Definitely, definitely.
Just not to you. Or you.
Or...where are you going?
Oh, right. Perhaps if...
No?
Ok, I see.
I do see.
I see now.
I'm sorry.
That's the truth.

I try

Your voice is new to me
but your scruffy giggle is all too familiar.
Your eyes aren't mine and yet I goosepimple
when they widen at another pair the same age aimed at you;
your mouth curling coy and hesitant.
Your face is a beautiful bad liar.
I try not to see me in you.
I try.

But I see the impatience in your hands,
hear the frustration on your tongue.
The bubbling will and intention the size of a moon
pulling the swirls of curiosity carelessly and dangerously
into a charged wave that fills your chest, head and arms
and explodes through your clumsy,
awkward, beautiful actions
and I know that you feel that exquisite energy
that burns alive.

But I see what burns ahead.
I see the rocks to stumble upon
and the bruises that may not heal.
I see the damage that stays.
Those dead ends that build brick walls
that keep you safe and lonely.
I see the deep hole to fill with hollow things.
I see the time lost in not seeing.

And I can't show you the rocks
because your rocks will be different.
And I can't guide you from the flames
because burning teaches you about fire.

And I can't stop you pushing dangerously ahead
because I see that big bright burning
energy fizzing through your fingers
and I see myself before the bruises and before the burns.
Before the deep hole you filled.

Sewn in

My Nana sewed and knitted at nights and weekends.
She let out the waists of neighbours
and took in the hems of family -
the clacking motor of her Singer sewing machine
whirring into the night.

By day she'd weft and warp the floor
of the haberdashery department of Fenwicks,
where she sold the tools of a trade her fingers were born for
but a marriage to a proud, unchangeable man denied her.

The city's sewers, stitchers and knitters
took their tools from her hands -
to stitch up the tears she didn't.
To patch up the holes she couldn't.
Newcastle, it seemed, needed a lot of mending.

For ten years she stitched up my tears
and patched up my holes.
I'd steal her elastic to make crossbows.
I'd borrow her hedgehog pin cushion
to put in my sister's bed.
She'd exact her revenge by knitting me Arran jumpers,
by making me thread her needles,
by forcing me to feed material through her machine -
her clacking motor never ceasing, always whirring.
Until the whirring stopped.

The machine was put in a box and placed out of sight.
Hems and waistbands stayed unaltered,
tears unsewed, patches unstitched.

But I can thread a needle
and my holes and tears do not stay unpatched.
The skin I wear does not stay unaltered.
My clothes can change to fit wherever I go.
I am not bound to where I started,
to where anyone wishes me to stay.

But a place can thread a needle
and places can sew and weave.
And wherever I go, I know when I return
I can be part of the fabric that mends.

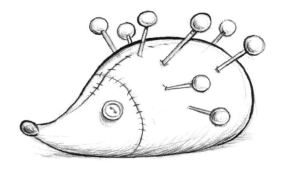

The greatest poem never written

This will be the greatest written piece of my career.
It will be bold, fearless, unapologetic and cut-throat incisive.
It will transcend and eclipse any previous attempts to…
"Dad, what will I wear when I grow up?"
"Wear? You can wear whatever you like."
"I don't want to wear your clothes."
"You don't have to."
"That's good."

This piece will connect on a level previously unparalleled in
prior literary creativity commanding the kind of awe-inspired
respect not seen since…
"Are you putting the kettle on, Scott?"
"I wasn't. Do you want me to?"
"Could I have tea please?"

…awe-inspired respect not seen since the likes of the romantic
poets but with the contemporary and cavalier edge of the beat
generation in its…
"Are you busy?"
"Yes, actually."
"It's just I've missed the bus to my Dad's and it wasn't my
fault because I was at Becca's and she doesn't have a watch and
I didn't have the time 'cos my phone needs charging but the
charger's at my dad's even though he says he hasn't got it but I
know he has because Amanda was the last person to use it and
I told her to put it back in my bedroom but I bet she's taken it
to work…"
"I'll get my shoes on."

Where were we? Contemporary, cavalier, edgy. Yes, edgy like
the beat generation. Like the punk poets. Like the 'Fuck you I'll
say whatever the fuck I like to whoever the fuck I want...'
"Fuh...Uh...Cuh..."
"What?!"
"What's that word, Dad?"
"It's bedtime!"
"Can I have a story?"
"'Yes, of course."

Right...what the fuck was I writing? Punk poets. Why punk
poets? Oh yeah. This thing will shine with grit and grubby
honesty, with a knife edge that cuts relentlessly through...
"Can I just..."
"What?"
"No, it's fine. I'll do it later."
"What is it?"
"I just need to get on my email. Can you save what you're
doing?"
"Fine."
"I'm done."
"Good."

Right. A relentless bloody knife cutting through the...
"Can somebody wipe me bum please?!"
...shit.
"Ok, do you want to flush?"
"Yes, shall we wash our hands with the blue soap?"
"Yes. Good night little man. Love you."
"Love you too, Dad."

This poem will be,
may be, could be,
the greatest written piece there has ever been.
But it would mean far less than the bits between.